YOU CAN HELP SOMEONE WHO'S GRIEVING

A How-To Healing Handbook

Victoria Frigo, Diane Fisher &
Mary Lou Cook

Penguin Books

PENGUIN BOOKS
Published by the Penguin Group
Penguin Books USA Inc., 375 Hudson Street,
New York, New York 10014, U.S.A.
Penguin Books Ltd, 27 Wrights Lane,
London W8 5TZ, England
Penguin Books Australia Ltd, Ringwood,
Victoria, Australia
Penguin Books Canada Ltd, 10 Alcorn Avenue,
Toronto, Ontario, Canada M4V 3B2
Penguin Books (N.Z.) Ltd, 182–190 Wairau Road,
Auckland 10, New Zealand

Penguin Books Ltd, Registered Offices:
Harmondsworth, Middlesex, England

First published in Penguin Books 1996

1 3 5 7 9 10 8 6 4 2

ISBN 0 14 02.5907 4

CIP data available

Printed in the United States of America
Set in Palatino

You Can Help Someone
Who's Grieving

For Scott

because he provided the experience

Foreword

Everyone grieves; it is part of our human experience to do so. Our goal must be to grieve wisely, honestly, and consciously, and not to avoid or hide from grief.

Because grief is universal, this book by Frigo, Fisher, and Cook is extremely important. These authors guide us gently through this difficult experience, and they show us how we can emerge stronger than before. This book is empathic and loving, because the authors know grieving firsthand. Because they have *lived* this book, through reading it their wisdom becomes ours.

At long last, our society is becoming increasingly willing to confront death, dying, and grieving, and Frigo, Fisher, and Cook are helping show the way. We cannot afford to turn away from these painful experiences, because we cannot be fully hunman unless we walk these paths. To wise guides such as these authors, let us be thankful.

Larry Dossey, M.D.
author of *Healing Words* and
Recovering the Soul

Barbara Dossey, R.N., M.S., F.A.A.N.
author of *Rituals of Healing* and
Holistic Nursing: A Handbook for Practice

Preface

We are a calligrapher, an entrepreneur, and a writer who came together sharing our experiences of loss and learning to form our own triad. Yes, we did make a book, but more important, we had the delight of working together.

Victoria Frigo, a writer and teacher, followed her path with MLC and Diane to help introduce these simple truths through prose.

After surviving the suicide of her son, Scott, Diane Fisher restructured her life toward helping others find a compassionate and creative direction for their own healing.

Mary Lou Cook (a.k.a. MLC) is a wise elder, designated Santa Fe Living Treasure, and a minister who lives committed to inner peace, forgiveness, and trust.

During the process of writing this book, we examined and shared our individual beliefs about death as transition. Although the three of us come from different religious and spiritual backgrounds, our personal journeys have led us to similar ideas.

We believe . . .

- ❖ A Universal Mind connects us all.
- ❖ The Spirit is in each of us.
- ❖ The Spirit is eternal.
- ❖ Death is only of the physical body.
- ❖ All pain and fear end for the deceased at the moment of death.
- ❖ Your loved one is not alone at the moment of death.
- ❖ After death, the Spirit contines on its journey.

Victoria Frigo

Diane Fisher

Mary Lou Cook

Santa Fe, New Mexico

Photo Credit: Santagto/Santa Fe

Acknowledgements

Deepest thanks to our collective angels, who provided continuous, loving support.

Contents

VIII. The Journey Continues

Introduction

This guidebook is about how you, as a friend, can help someone who's grieving. It contains common sense thoughts about supporting survivors after the death of a loved one.

Speaking on behalf of those who are mourning, we present simple ideas on what's needed and suggestions on what you can do.

Acknowledging death enlarges us. Unfortunately, however, ours is a culture in which the experience of death is avoided and even denied. Alternatively, by accepting death as transition in our lives, we free ourselves of its power to terrorize us.

In grateful recognition of grieving, surviving, thriving, and flourishing, we offer this handbook.

You Can Help Someone Who's Grieving

This is an opportunity for you to make a difference.

I

Getting Involved in Grief Support

The Importance of Grieving

Healthy grieving, rather than unhealthy depression and despair, is good and necessary. Grieving is absolutely essential for both mental and physical wellness.

Denying feelings about death damages the immune system, causes reoccurring emotional difficulties, and blocks the survivor's ability to be happy. Tears of grief, on the other hand, cleanse the soul and restore the survivor's capacity to embrace life.

Grieving benefits survivors by deepening their understanding of life. These lessons can teach—

- ❖ Patience and acceptance
- ❖ Perspective and priorities
- ❖ Compassion and sensitivity
- ❖ The magnitude of feelings.

The Value of Your Presence

By "being present" for the survivor during her time of grief, you provide a rare and special gift of compassion. Many people would like to help after they hear about a death but don't know how. Sometimes, even good friends are at a loss as to what to say or do.

This handbook offers practical ideas and suggestions on how to "be present" for someone who's grieving. We all have the capacity to help each other connect in this human way.

Examining Your Own Feelings about Death

Prejudice isn't a word usually associated with death, but the term fits whenever it's suggested that one way of dying is better than another. For example, a death from AIDS or suicide may be judged more harshly than dying of old age—or the value of one life may be considered more "important" than another.

If you're extremely apprehensive about contacting the survivor, examine how you feel regarding the circumstances surrounding the death. You may be trying to avoid thoughts of your own mortality and the loss of others close to you. Resistance to change, fear of the unknown, and dread about dying are all natural.

Try to examine where your anxiety is coming from. Perhaps this is the time to embrace a philosophy that provides an enlightened outlook on living and dying.

Looking for Teachers

You may feel you don't have enough experience to handle the circumstances associated with death. But none of us has all the answers. Fortunately, you are surrounded by ordinary people who possess special wisdom based on their life experiences. These people can guide you on how to support a friend who's grieving.

Where do you find your teachers? Look around. Approach those who are good at handling difficult situations. Ask for their help. Using this method, you can gain a practical education taught by a faculty of brilliant people. We call this curriculum "intentional learning."

Remember to always acknowledge and thank the "teachers" who have supplemented your helping skills.

We Are All Creative

Every situation following death is different. At times, you will need to be creative and flexible while helping the survivor. By "creative" we don't mean artistic talent. We mean using your imagination and inventiveness to solve problems in new ways.

Every person is born with creativity, but not all of us know how to utilize it. Contact a creative person who's demonstrated common sense and contentment. Present the situation, and then look for answers in brainstorming. You'll see how quickly it works.

Some wonderful benefits are that you'll improve your outlook, you'll relax, and you'll see many new ways to solve problems.

Are You Interfering or Helping?

Some people hesitate to approach the survivor immediately following the death. They feel their help may not be needed or they may be in the way.

Rather than guessing at what would be best, check in with the grieving person and simply ask, "Can I help or am I interfering?" You can use the same approach to find out what the survivor wants. For example, you could ask, "Do you feel like talking about the death?"

Reassure the survivor that you're OK with whatever she says. Later, however, you may want to repeat these questions. Survivors require varying amounts of support and stability, and as their circumstances change, so do their needs.

Our lives are shaped by those
who leave as much as by those who remain.

II

Practical Helping

❖　❖　❖

Immediately Following the Death

The first days following the death are filled with loss, shock, and disbelief. During this time, however, important obligations and functions must be performed.

As soon as you hear the news, contact the survivor and extend your support. If you can, offer to call any special people the grieving person would like to have close by at this time. Find out what the survivor would like you to say to them about the death.

To help even more, be prepared with a notebook and pencil to start getting things organized:

- ❖ Make sure the proper authorities have been called to care for the body.
- ❖ List everyone to be notified.
- ❖ Write down all telephone messages completely.
- ❖ Keep track of visitors and their kind gestures.
- ❖ Jot down household routines that must be attended to—

Errands	Laundry
Children's schedules	House cleaning
Pet and plant care	Yard work
Meals	Kitchen crew

- ❖ Throughout the day, gently encourage the survivor to rest and take some nourishment.

So Much to Do

Very shortly after the death, the survivor may need help—

- ❖ Writing the obituary (We suggest publishing it for 3 consecutive days.)
- ❖ Deciding on the memorial service
- ❖ Being driven around
- ❖ Setting up a calendar for meals, errands, and other household tasks and delegating assignments from this calendar
- ❖ Adding to the list of people to be notified
- ❖ Offering hospitality to visitors.

As a special friend, you could add the following to your personal to-do list:

- ❖ Give the grieving person a ruled journal. In the midst of the turmoil, it's good therapy to have a place to write private feelings.

- Make sure that someone is always actively present for the survivor.
- Pay attention to how the death may be affecting other family members.

Funerals and Memorial Services

Funerals or memorial services bring meaningful closure by celebrating and honoring the life of the deceased.

A funeral is a traditional ceremony of burial centered around a casket or cremation urn. Funerals are almost always organized and held in churches or funeral homes.

Memorial services are generally planned by family and friends—and can be located in any favorite place—indoors or outdoors.

Depending on the survivor's preference, funeral or memorial services may offer family and friends opportunities for creative and personal involvement

- ❖ Performing special music
- ❖ Sharing stories
- ❖ Reciting favorite passages
- ❖ Displaying photographs or personal items
- ❖ Playing audio or visual recordings
- ❖ Reading letters and telegrams.

Outline of a Sample Memorial Service

Based on a ceremony performed by
The Reverend Mary Lou Cook

1. **Recognize the value of rituals to heal us.**
   "We meet together today to honor and speak of our dear
   _____. We need these rituals, these rites of passage, for beginnings and endings. We need each other, and we need to acknowledge our feelings of grief, loss, pain, and hurt. It's OK to weep. In fact, it's encouraged. Our tears are healing."

2. **Acknowledge your appreciation of everyone present.**
   "Your presence is a tribute to _____. Thank you."

3. **Signify the importance of this occasion with a simple ceremony.**
   "We will light four candles for _____ and for ourselves. We light one for grief, one for our courage, one for our memories, and one for our love."

4. **Discuss what death teaches us.**

   "Life and death bring questions and answers. Why are we here? Who are we? We are here to bless the world, not change it. We are here to forgive, to love, to heal, to be kind, to acknowledge everyone as our brothers and sisters, to attain release from fear, to search for the spiritual, and, in doing so, to choose our path."

5. **Suggest ways to keep the memory of the deceased alive in our lives.**

   "Yes, _____ is gone from our sight but not from our lives and hearts. We start our grieving and healing by asking friends for support and comfort. We write poetry about _____, we plant a tree in his name, we mentor a young person in his name, we endow a project in his name, we give to (his favorite charity) in his name, we do kind deeds in his name."

6. **Share stories (photos, recordings, other memorabilia) of the deceased.**

7. Ask for a blessing.

"Our hearts are broken. Oh, God of Comfort!"

"Give us healing. Give us peace. Give us acceptance. Give us hope, and help us trust again."

The Board of Directors

- ❖ Insurance questions
- ❖ Financial decisions
- ❖ Legal matters
- ❖ Household maintenance
- ❖ Family mediation

During this overwhelming time, you can suggest a new idea patterned after a corporate "Board of Directors." This "Board of Directors" creates a support system of volunteers who help the survivor with decisions. "Board" members should reflect a wide range of specialties. What they have in common is a positive attitude and a willingness to share their advice for the best interest of the survivor.

Let's Get Material

It happens in almost every family. Legal, material, or financial issues following a death create dissension and hurt feelings. Even personal possessions that may not seem to be of any value can mean a lot. Often, the haggling over these objects causes lifelong divisions.

If the person who died has failed to leave a will or final instructions, you can offer to help in this sticky situation. Volunteer to serve as an impartial arbitrator by devising a method that allows everyone a turn in choosing personal items. In fairness to each person, keep a list of who gets what.

And remember, flexibility and humor are indispensable in working toward a harmonious mediation.

Thank You Notes

Often survivors either wear themselves out or dread the obligation of writing thank you notes. You might suggest that it is quite acceptable for the survivor to send printed copies of an original, hand-written "thanks." Only a few lines are necessary.

The staff at a copy center will provide directions on how to print the notes and suggest a variety of paper and envelopes. This project can be organized quickly and inexpensively, especially with the help of friends.

The greatest responsibility
of all who love—is to listen.

III

Showing Your Support

Supportive Listening

L istening is the most important aspect of "being present."

Take responsibility for finding a time and place to listen. Block out distractions. Focus directly on the one who is grieving as he pours out his feelings and vents his emotions. Listen with your eyes and heart so he knows he has your complete attention and acceptance.

This is not a time to voice your own opinions. Merely nodding affirms the grieving person's words.

The Value of a Hug

Sometimes you just don't know what to say or do to comfort the survivor. Fortunately, words aren't always necessary. A hug often takes the place of words and transfers loving energy. Hugs come in many forms and intensities—from a tender, gentle experience to a painful, rib-breaking ordeal.

Gently reach out to see if the grieving person will accept this gesture. Not everyone is accustomed to receiving a hug, but it's the best we humans have come up with.

Words a Survivor May Not Be Ready to Hear

- ❖ "It's God's will."
- ❖ "You'll get over this."
- ❖ "Time will heal."
- ❖ "Keep busy."
- ❖ "Be strong."
- ❖ "You have another child."
- ❖ "At least he didn't suffer."
- ❖ "Now she's at peace."
- ❖ "He's in a better place."
- ❖ "Something good will come of this."
- ❖ "Try not to think about it."
- ❖ "Don't cry."
- ❖ "It's time to move on."
- ❖ "You should be over this by now."

- ❖ "It's a blessing."
- ❖ "When are you going back to work?"
- ❖ and many, many more . . .

These overused phrases, although well-intentioned, can often cause anger and confusion. Be sensitive and thoughtful in the words you choose.

Thoughtful Words

Although many people might think it's better not to dwell on the survivor's sadness, it actually seems to lighten the sorrow if you acknowledge the pain and loss. You might say—

- ❖ "I'm sorry."
- ❖ "I care."
- ❖ "I wish you peace."
- ❖ "I know your heart is broken."
- ❖ "I wish I could share your pain."
- ❖ "I know you're hurting."
- ❖ "I'm here for you."

The "D" Word

Because death and extinction are our greatest fears, we avoid using the words "death" and "dying." We replace them with euphemisms such as "passed over," "passed away," "left us," or "gone."

Don't be afraid to use the "D" word with the survivor. This encourages honest dialogue about fears associated with death and helps release the power that death holds over us. Acknowledging our mortality is the driving force that causes us to look for deeper answers.

Supporting Decisions

Decision-making is often difficult, but it is especially complex for a survivor during the period of grief. The survivor may be filled with self-doubt. Sometimes he is torn between the shoulds, oughts, and musts, on the one hand, and what his heart would really like to do, on the other.

You can help the survivor by encouraging him to examine his authentic feelings. Once his decision has been made, give him your loyal support. Assure the grieving person that others' opinions are not relevant. "There's no right way. There's no wrong way. There's only your way."

Writing a Note of Sympathy

Survivors cherish sympathy notes that contain feelings from the heart, anecdotes, admired traits, and reflections about how the deceased person touched your life.

To gather your thoughts, simply jot down what you remember about the one who died. Think about his favorite activities, or places. If you let your mind relax, the right words will come.

Now you're ready to begin writing the actual letter.

> ❖ Start by expressing your sympathy. (It's OK to refer to the death, but you needn't dwell on it.)
> ❖ Mention some personal reminiscence.
> ❖ If you sincerely want to do more, state your desire to help.
> ❖ End with a thought for the survivor's comfort and peace.

Sympathy notes assure the grieving person that you empathize with his loss and the deceased will be remembered.

In Lieu of Flowers

Because flowers are Nature's gift of beauty and poetry, they are one of the most traditional ways of expressing sympathy. But sometimes another type of tribute is preferred, such as a donation to a charity. This request is printed in the obituary notice or discussed among friends of the deceased.

Even if the survivor has not mentioned it, a personal and creative expression of sympathy in lieu of flowers is always appropriate.

In honor of the deceased you could—

> ❖ Make a financial donation to a worthy cause
> ❖ Establish a scholarship fund
> ❖ Plant a tree
> ❖ Make a quilt
> ❖ Burn a 7-day candle
> ❖ Create a scrapbook
> ❖ Donate a book to the library
> ❖ Write a poem
> ❖ Construct a small shrine
> ❖ Volunteer for a community service project.

In a dark time, the eye begins to see.

IV

The Most-Asked Question

Is There a God?

The survivor may say: "Is there a God?" "Why did God do this?" "Why has God abandoned me?"

These words signal a desire for spiritual understanding. They are the beginning of the survivor's journey toward some resolution about death and a deeper meaning of life. You can assist the grieving person in his search for personal answers by providing literature or tapes from inspired writers.

If you haven't any idea about what to suggest, remain open to being guided, and TRUST. You will find the right material.

Every journey begins with a farewell.

V

Insights Into the Survivor's Grief

What Is Grief?

- The feeling of infinite sorrow
- Eternal separation
- Crushing emptiness
- Wrenching loss
- Unfillable void
- That nothing, nothing matters
- Why? Why? Why?
- Vague confusion
- That nothing will ever be the same
- That life has lost its meaning
- Deep despair
- Profound loneliness
- Irrational fear that you also are dying
- Unrelenting sadness
- Devastating numbness
- Missing the physical presence

Expect the survivor to suffer these waves of emotions as a normal part of grieving. One touch of kindness with understanding may help ease the pain. At times, that's all you can do.

How Long Will the Grieving Last?

Well-meaning friends may offer opinions about when the grieving should be over. Assure the survivor that none of these estimates matter. Encourage him to take as long as he needs to heal. Let him follow his own timetable, not anyone else's.

Most experts say that the normal phases of grieving include denial, anger, bargaining, depression, and acceptance. A person may enter and reenter any of these stages in any order for various lengths of time.

Each individual grieves until he's finished.

Changes

Sometime after the loss, you may notice changes in the survivor's usual behavior. Perhaps the death will start the grieving person on an inner journey of unprecedented evolution. The survivor might—

- ❖ Lose interest in previously fulfilling work
- ❖ Distance herself in relationships
- ❖ Explore new life-styles
- ❖ Re-evaluate her life's purpose.

Recognize that your relationship with the survivor could change as well.

Anger

The survivor may express anger in various ways:

- ❖ Chilly silence
- ❖ Irrational outbursts
- ❖ Physical violence
- ❖ Sarcasm and cynicism
- ❖ Self-inflicted punishment and guilt
- ❖ Suppressed feelings
- ❖ Uneasy tension.

It's normal in grieving for the survivor to have these feelings, but keeping anger inside is destructive. Instead, offer to talk about it. Insights may reveal that we're not always angry for the reason we think.

Depression

- ❖ Lack of energy
- ❖ Inability to focus
- ❖ Not wanting to get out of bed
- ❖ Negative outlook
- ❖ Irrational fears and guilt
- ❖ Disinterest in personal appearance
- ❖ Forgetfulness
- ❖ Continuous crying
- ❖ Eating disorders
- ❖ Obsessive behavior
- ❖ No interest in anything
- ❖ Fear of insanity
- ❖ Withdrawal

Watch for signs of depression in the survivor. A certain amount of this behavior is appropriate for healthy grieving, but depression over extended time merits attention. If you notice the grieving person not moving through these phases, suggest a check-up or professional guidance.

Death's Other Losses

In addition to the death, related losses will surface for the survivor. Be prepared for this other dimension of grieving to unfold as part of the aftermath.

The survivor may also lose—

- ❖ Companionship
- ❖ Security
- ❖ Sense of immortality
- ❖ Routine
- ❖ Innocence
- ❖ Hopes and dreams
- ❖ Wise counsel.

Forgiving the One Who Has Died

The survivor may be holding onto a grudge toward the one who has died—a feeling justified because of abusive, addictive, or thoughtless behavior.

We're born not knowing how to forgive. Forgiving is a learned response—something we have to work at. Holding a grudge is destructive to mental and physical health. You can suggest that the survivor write it down on paper, tear it up, and burn it or flush it away.

We need to forgive God, others, circumstances and events—and, especially, ourselves. Forgiveness is the way to happiness and peace.

Unfinished Business

After the death, the survivor may feel remorse and guilt about having lost the chance forever to set things right. But, the truth is, there's still an opportunity. Following the death, many people experience the spiritual presence of the one who died.

During this powerful time, you can suggest that the survivor pay attention to "signs." They could serve as an important opening to make peace—by writing a letter, keeping a journal, or communicating silently through conversations or dreams.

A Page for Youth

For the young survivor, death causes feelings of abandonment. Often, young people experience guilt, because they believe they provoked the death by doing something wrong. In spite of these emotions, children may not express their feelings immediately.

In explaining the death, choose your words carefully. Referring to the deceased as "sleeping" or "gone away" may cause the child needless worry about his own security. Listen to the child with special understanding and patience. Reassure the young person that he is guiltless. Promise to respect confidences shared with you. Next, speak with an empathetic representative from the child's school. Perhaps the school can create a peer grief support group guided by a professional facilitator.

Over time, pay attention to the child's emotional and physical health. If the child seems unwell, gently suggest to the family that the young person may need professional assistance.

A Page for Men

Be aware of the cultural conflicts that men feel when dealing with death and grieving. Erroneously, they are taught "men don't cry"—that feelings must be suppressed. At a time when men most need emotional release, they may appear unapproachable. Realize that this distancing is really a call for help. Since the answer to every need is compassion, respond compassionately.

Try to gain understanding. Offer: "How can I help?" "What do you want me to do?" or "I want to listen to you."

Acknowledge the courage it takes for a man to express his feelings openly.

A Page for Women

Encourage women to honor their powers. Feminine qualities such as sensitivity, vulnerability, and intuition are very helpful in coping with grief. You can provide a safe place for women to express their feelings and begin the healing process. Although feminine behavior often is dismissed as weak, actually it is a source of strength. During the grief process these qualities can serve as a model of how to mourn.

*Know there is a place in you
where nothing is impossible.*

VI

Helping Survivors Survive

Letting Go

Letting go means allowing the one who has died to leave and continue on her journey. To achieve healing, the grieving person will need to "let go" again and again in many different ways. Be aware that these last goodbyes are some of the hardest things a person will ever do.

It is not your job to suggest that the survivor "let go." Rather, recognize the difficulty of trying to say goodbye. Offer your gentle support. If you have the opportunity, reassure the survivor that "letting go" doesn't mean forgetting.

Keeping a Journal

A good gift for the grieving person is a blank, ruled book to use as a journal. A journal offers a place to pour out feelings and record emotional progress over time.

If the survivor needs some hints on how to begin, suggest—

- ❖ Setting aside uninterrupted time
- ❖ Writing about the grief
- ❖ Recording dreams
- ❖ Beginning a sentence with "I'm remembering . . ." To get unstuck, repeat "I'm remembering . . ."
- ❖ Writing rapidly for 5 to 10 minutes without lifting the pen from the page. This connects with the subconscious.

Keeping a journal is easy. No one else reads the entries, so the author can say anything he chooses. And the writing doesn't have to be perfect. In fact, it can be the worst stuff in America!

Support Groups

Support groups are composed of people from all walks of life who meet to share common experiences. There may come a time when the survivor is ready for the unique understanding found in a support group.

To help the survivor locate an appropriate group, consult the local—

- ❖ Library
- ❖ Newspaper calendar
- ❖ Church
- ❖ Funeral home
- ❖ Hospice center
- ❖ Police headquarters
- ❖ Hospital.

Offer to accompany the survivor to the first meeting. If he cannot find a group that suits his needs, contact a few kindred spirits and help them start their own support group. Being with others who have experienced similar losses nurtures healing.

Holidays and Anniversaries

Some holidays or anniversaries after the death are especially painful. The survivor may choose to continue past traditions or adopt nontraditional ways to "just get through it." Even if no one else understands, encourage the survivor to take care of himself rather than succumb to holiday pressures.

Some alternative ideas for observing special days include—

- ❖ Working in a soup kitchen during a holiday meal
- ❖ Sharing a birthday cake with a day care center
- ❖ Taking a trip
- ❖ Going on a retreat
- ❖ Initiating a new friendship
- ❖ Escaping to a movie or into a book.

Or, if the survivor doesn't feel like it, he can give himself permission not to celebrate.

Hope, Humor, and Miracles

In the midst of sadness and loss, it's easy to forget the values that help us get through.

- ❖ Ask the survivor to take a nature walk with you. Seeing signs that life goes on restores hope.
- ❖ Welcome humor into the situation. Laughing helps cope with the pain.
- ❖ Remind the survivor that we're entitled to miracles every day, but we tend to block them. Expect good things to happen. Trust the Universe.

Everyone we have truly loved
is a part of us.

VII

Special Considerations

Was There Time to Say Goodbye?

A death that was anticipated will affect survivors differently than a sudden, unanticipated loss. Throughout prolonged illnesses, such as AIDS or other terminal diseases, people frequently begin to grieve prior to the death. Their reactions at a funeral may be very different than survivors who have suffered the unexpected loss of a loved one. For example, accidents and violent assaults often deny survivors the chance to say goodbye.

Be sensitive to the diverse reactions of survivors based on the circumstances surrounding the death.

Death of a Child

It's out of the natural order for a child to die before a parent. Certain dynamics exist in this unthinkable situation. Friends hesitate to come forward because of their fears that they, too, could suffer such a loss. Be aware of your own fears. In addition, reassure the parents that guilt is a normal factor in grief. Do what you can to let the family know that they did the best they could.

People who can really help are others who have lost a child. Therefore, locate a Compassionate Friends group (a nationwide organization) in your area, and ask a member to contact the survivors.

Death of an Unborn Child

It's important to acknowledge and honor the painful loss to someone who has experienced a miscarriage or abortion. She often feels emptiness and disappointment with unfulfilled dreams for the tiny spirit.

Some suggestions you may offer the survivor to help bring closure and peace include—

❖ Writing a love letter to the unborn child
❖ Speaking silently to the child's spirit
❖ Creating a quiet ceremony.

Suicide

In addition to the longing and sorrow that is a natural part of grieving, survivors of suicide experience profound guilt, shame, abandonment, and regret. Their pain is further intensified by cultural and religious stigmas that continue to surround the act.

Your sensitivity to the unique problems faced by survivors of suicide will help:

- ❖ Listen compassionately. Allow the survivor to talk and talk and talk in an atmosphere of safe acceptance.
- ❖ Absolutely do not make any moral judgments about the deceased or the act. In order to do this, you'll need to work through your own beliefs and attitudes about suicide.
- ❖ Keep in your heart the gift of the deceased person's entire life rather than his final moments.

- Help with the physical aftermath of suicide.
- Offer to accompany the grieving person to a suicide support group meeting. Survivors find it healing to be surrounded by others who have experienced the same kind of loss.

Trust the Universe in all that happens.

VIII

The Journey Continues

Healing Prescriptions

When the time seems appropriate, you may want to share this list with the survivor to remind her to take care of herself.

Dear Survivor,

You've been through a lot. Here are some ways to be kind to yourself.

- ❖ Visualize feeling healthy and hold this picture in your mind.
- ❖ Play soothing music (for example, nature sounds or meditative chants).
- ❖ Pamper yourself with a hot soak.
- ❖ Turn off the violence. Avoid newspapers and TV.
- ❖ Surround yourself with kind and nurturing friends. Distance yourself from difficult people.
- ❖ Eliminate unnecessary stress.
- ❖ Share your compassion with someone else.
- ❖ Join a support group of kindred spirits.
- ❖ Learn how to meditate.

- ❖ Keep a journal of your feelings.
- ❖ Participate in pleasureable exercise, preferably outdoors.
- ❖ Eat nutritious foods and drink lots of water.
- ❖ Practice deep and cleansing breathing.
- ❖ Get a gentle massage.
- ❖ Rest and nap.
- ❖ Allow yourself to experience humor.
- ❖ Choose to live in peace rather than fear.

Vaya Con Diós

Our intention has been to be a part of the understanding, healing, and peace of the Universe. We hope this book has given you the support you need to help those in your life who are grieving.

For further information about grief support provided by Diane Fisher, please send a self-addressed stamped envelope to—

Diane Fisher
P.O. Box 550692
Atlanta, GA 30355